A PERSO

MW01527535

PERSONAL PRAYERS
IN
TIMES OF GRIEF

Brief prayers of comfort and hope
for people who are facing
personal grief

JUDITH AND MICHAEL
MURRAY

DIMENSIONS
FOR LIVING
NASHVILLE

PERSONAL PRAYERS IN TIMES OF GRIEF

Originally published under the title Personal Grieving, *Copyright © 1989 Openbook Publishers, 205 Halifax Street, Adelaide, South Australia*

Dimensions for Living edition published 2003

This book is printed on recycled, acid-free, elemental chlorine–free paper.

ISBN 0-687-07398-7

Scripture quotations are from The Good News Bible: Today's English Version (TEV). © 1976 by the American Bible Society.

03 04 05 06 07 08 09 10 11 12—10 9 8 7 6 5 4 3 2 1

MANUFACTURED IN THE UNITED STATES OF AMERICA

Grief Is a Result of a Loss

When we grieve we all have to face our own particular problem in our own unique way. Each experience will have certain unique characteristics. Yet all of us share one thing in common: we share grief.

The dictionary defines *grief* as "deep and evident sorrow." Grief is a natural reaction to losing something important. All of us who grieve suffer because we have lost something precious to us. What we have lost may differ, and the intensities of our grief also differ. Yet we all experience the deep sorrow of grief.

Some suffer the loss of a dear one. It may be a husband, a wife, a parent, a child, or a friend. Others grieve because they have lost their familiar home or their job. Still others lose their dream for the future; a door is closed, and what they hoped for is no longer possible.

Whatever your loss, you, like all of us, have to suffer.

Heavenly Father, you love me so much that you gave your Son to die for me. Be with me in my grief. Amen.

Your Own Pain Hurts You the Most

Some losses may produce more intense, more prolonged grief than others. It is pointless to try to compare the grief of one person with that of another. Suffering is not something to be measured and compared, like the size of a house or the cost of a car.

Suffering hurts, and your suffering hurts you. It doesn't make any difference that another's grief is deeper or more justified in the eyes of others. Grief is a very unique experience. Your grief hurts you more than the grief of others, because it is happening to you. A person may sympathize with another's pain, but to you your pain is greater, simply because you feel it. Other people's pain is happening to them. It won't mean as much to you as your own.

This is not meant to be selfish or cruel. It is meant to help us realize that it is acceptable to feel our pain, even if others around us feel that it is unwarranted.

Lord, sometimes I feel very lonely. Help me find comfort in the knowledge that you understand and share my pain. Amen.

You Have the Right to Your Own Sorrow

It is natural to feel grief over a loss. Normally, if they are allowed to be experienced and expressed initially, these deep feelings will ease with time. Meanwhile, your pain is real.

People who suffer a loss are sometimes told: "You'll get over it," or "It's all for the best," or "At least you don't have to suffer like _____," or "Snap out of it! Life has to go on."

Comments like these, while perhaps containing an element of truth, are inappropriate because they deny the right of the bereaved to feel and express their grief in their own way. They may then feel guilty about their feelings and attempt to suppress them, instead of experiencing the pain and coming to terms with it. Such reactions can lead to problems.

Understanding a little about the grief we are experiencing can help us cope with it by removing some of the fear of the unknown.

Heavenly Lord, I cannot hide my feelings of hurt from you. Stand by me in my time of trouble. Amen.

Our Past Affects Our Experience of Grief

The grief we experience through our own particular loss is very real. How we cope with that grief will be very individual. We do not enter this difficult period of grieving devoid of a past and a background.

Many factors will affect our journey through grief. Some people have a relatively smooth, direct journey, while the journey of others will be continually thwarted with delays and detours. Unfortunately, some even fail to reach their destination, and their unresolved grief may disrupt their lives for many years.

We shall look at some of the factors that vary among individuals, and thus may influence their grief in differing ways.

One vital factor is the emotional investment involved. In general, the more dependent the bereaved was on a loved one, the more intense the grief caused by the loss will tend to be. Those who have seen their whole life revolving around their loved one may find their grief complicated by a loss of meaning and direction in their life.

Lord, give me the strength to face my loss. Remind me that your love will never leave me. Amen.

Previous Life Experiences

How we deal with any stressful situations in our lives is affected largely by the way we have dealt with stress in the past. From childhood, we have developed our own particular means of coping with stress.

We can see different reactions to difficult situations in children. One child who falls off a horse may get angry and strike the horse. Another may cry and run away, whereas yet another may seek help and get right back on the horse.

Adults react to painful situations in similar, yet uniquely individual ways. We all know people who "run away" from problems, or who "explode," or who "analyze" everything, or who "go into their shell."

In our current trials we will tend to react as we have to previous crises. Some means of coping are more effective than others in allowing us to work through the problem. If an individual has not developed effective coping skills, crises may not be resolved. These experiences may then affect future crises, making them even more complicated and trying.

Lord, guide me in the most effective way of coping with my grief. Amen.

Preparation for the Loss

How we cope with a loss can be affected by whether or not we have had time to prepare for a loss.

For example, relatives of the terminally ill know of their coming loss beforehand, and thus are given a time during which they can prepare for their loss. If this preparation phase is worked through successfully, some of the stress of the final parting can be alleviated. In a sense, they can begin their grieving gradually. This is not to say that the loss will not still be accompanied by numbing sorrow when it actually happens.

On the other hand, a sudden death, such as in a car accident, leaves the relatives initially in deep shock and without any psychological readiness to grieve. Such unexpected losses can also occur in childbirth situations such as miscarriage, stillbirth, and the birth of a child with a disability. Suddenly one's whole life changes drastically.

Some period of preparatory grief before the actual event *may* help a person cope with the final loss, but this is not always the case.

Lord Jesus Christ, you are Lord of life and death, and you are my Lord. Remind me of your constant love for me. Amen.

Life-Situation and Personality Factors

Various personality factors can affect how we cope with a loss.

Males and females may differ in their reactions. Their differing perspectives on life, their hormonal differences, and their conditioning as children may affect their reactions.

Age can also be a factor. Older people may be less flexible. On the other hand, they may have lived through more disappointments, and, in coping with these, they may have developed a maturity born out of crisis.

The personality of the bereaved can also affect the process of grief. A person who inhibits feelings or is prone to feelings of guilt may cope less effectively than one who is openly expressive and self-confident.

We have little control over most of these factors, but knowing about them can help us understand what is happening. Then it may not be quite so frightening for us.

Lord, help me understand myself and put my trust in you. Amen.

FAITH IN A GOOD AND WISE GOD

Our religious beliefs can also strongly affect our grief. A belief in the goodness, love, and wisdom of God can help us accept our loss as part of a plan, even though we cannot fully understand it. Hence we are provided with meaning in a seemingly senseless situation.

On the other hand, those without faith in God may see their loss as simply fate or bad luck in a cold and meaningless universe. Those who see their loss as the punishment of a harsh God, or who feel under pressure to "prove" the strength of their faith in their crisis, may also face added difficulty.

Those who must also face other crises at the same time—such as financial worries, other bereavements, or unemployment or difficulties at work—are at a further disadvantage.

Heavenly Lord, I know that because of your Son you have accepted me as your dear child. Reassure me of your loving care for me. Amen.

Who Is to Blame?

As human beings we like to believe that there is a cause for every incident—so that when things go wrong there is something or someone to blame. We tend to find it unacceptable that God and nature do not follow our rules. We look for someone to blame for our troubles, and will even accept the blame ourselves.

If bereaved people are able, rightly or wrongly, to attribute blame to themselves, they may experience more intense feelings of guilt and depression caused by a turning in of anger on themselves. Such anger may be difficult to alleviate through rational discussion. Often the loss of confidence and sense of failure that accompany these feelings of guilt are difficult emotions to deal with. The bereaved may tend to feel that those attempting to help are "just being nice," while covering up the blame and anger they really feel.

In some cases, the bereaved feel anger and resentment toward others—perhaps the doctor, a relative, or God, or even the lost loved one.

Lord Jesus Christ, you have died to take away our sin and guilt. Relieve me of feelings of guilt and resentment. Amen.

Support from Family and Friends

Grieving is essentially a journey we must travel alone. However, the support available to us during our grief can greatly affect the passage and outcome of the process. The type of support offered varies.

A bereaved person is fortunate if he or she has a marriage partner who shares the experience. The couple who cry together, who comfort each other, and who together mourn their loss, are one.

Family and friends can also prove vital sources of support. Many bereaved people are protected under a strong umbrella of loving concern opened about them by family and friends. Unfortunately, others may not encounter this so readily. Distance or death may have separated the bereaved from their closest family members and friends. An inability to understand the feelings of the bereaved or to cope with any stressful situation may lead some family and friends to avoid these unpleasant situations, and hence also avoid the bereaved.

Times of loss often lead to a reevaluation of friendships.

Heavenly Lord, help me always remember that you never leave me, and that you always understand me. Amen.

Support from Church and Society

The wider society and the church can provide further support for us in grief. This support may come from doctors, nurses, professional counselors, support groups, our priest or minister, and fellow members of the congregation. These people can provide us with information, understanding, and friendship.

In some cases, hospitals and doctors have developed specific strategies of support for those suffering loss. However, many support facilities depend on the suffering person seeking out their assistance. For many people, finding the confidence and courage to do this while grieving or depressed is difficult. Recognizing that someone is not coping successfully is less likely in today's highly mobile, urban society.

The church as the family of faith and the bearer of the message of God's love, can often be a real help— although church members are also human and may not always recognize or know how to deal with the need.

Thank you, Lord, for providing human instruments of comfort and help. Amen.

GRIEF IS HARD WORK

People often say that grief must be "worked through." Yet only those who have faced grief can fully accept how apt that phrase really is. Grief is work, hard work—perhaps the hardest work we may have to face in life.

Grief can't be avoided indefinitely. It stands as a wall between us and our future peace of mind. It is a wall that must eventually be demolished if we are ever to regain some semblance of peace in our lives.

Some people meet the wall well equipped with bulldozers of support and effective coping skills. They demolish their wall of grief and emerge triumphant, even if bruised. Others are armed only with a shovel. They find the going difficult, but in time emerge triumphant also. Yet others attack their grief with their bare hands, emerging battered and exhausted. Some desperately run up and down, trying to find a way around, but finally they too must confront this obstacle.

However we tackle our grief, the way is not smooth, and from time to time we face setbacks.

Lord, be with me as I travel the ups and downs of my grief. Amen.

GRIEF CAN STRIKE ALL OF US

B elow are a few summary points about grief:

• Grief makes no consideration for age, sex, social status, religion, education, wealth or previous suffering. Suffering and grief can strike any of us at any time. Your time of grieving just happens to be now, in this situation. But you will not be alone; it comes to us all.

• Your reaction to grief has nothing to do with your intellect. You can't simply rationalize it away. It has to be confronted and experienced.

• Grief has its basis in our humanness. It is common to us all.

• Grief cannot be denied or ignored indefinitely. You may be able to repress it for a time, but it emerges in some way, such as in later illness.

• Grief is not pleasant or easy. It is senseless to try to hoodwink ourselves into believing that grief "isn't really all that bad." We don't like pain in our society, and prefer to avoid any possibly painful experience. Our inability to accept that grief is not pleasant or easy is reflected in the heavy use of tranquilizers prescribed for those experiencing grief, and in the conspicuous absence of support from some people who are unable to deal with another in pain.

Heavenly Lord, your Son suffered pain for us. Help me face and cope with my own suffering. Amen.

GRIEF IS AN INDIVIDUAL EXPERIENCE

Here are further points about grief:

• Grief is not a rational, logical process. More often it is like groping about in the dark, with no set pattern, looking for a light switch. It's like two steps forward and one back, with a nudge and a push off to the side. Our feelings during the grief may not be constant. Rather, there may be "up" and "down" days, the number of each type altering as grief is resolved.

• Grief is individual. It differs from person to person, family to family, and culture to culture. It does not have to follow some set pattern.

• Grief affects the whole person. Reactions can be seen in feelings of sadness, tiredness, hopelessness, anger, and guilt. The body, too, can show the pain the mind is confronting. Loss of muscular strength, stomach upset, shortness of breath, disturbed sleep, and muscle tightness are all common physical sensations of grief. We may also be absentminded, hyperactive, irritable, or careless.

• You can emerge from grief a stronger, more capable, more sensitive human being. Because of this, the pain of grief has actually been good for you, although at the time that is the last thing you want to be assured of!

Lord, I know that you watch over me and protect me, even in dark times. Help me trust in your loving care. Amen.

GRIEF IS A HEALING PROCESS

• It is impossible for one human being to understand fully another's grief. We can share grief, but there will always be parts of the journey that a person must travel alone. The journey can be made easier by others, but ultimately the final resolution is a personal experience.

• Grieving requires us to face our loss and accept it as reality.

• Grief can be compounded. Unresolved grief over a prior loss can complicate and deepen the grief of a new crisis.

• Grief need not be feared. It is a healthy means of coping with an incident in our lives that could otherwise destroy our peace of mind indefinitely. Grief is a form of healing. Like a broken leg, the loss is painful at first, but eventually the grief heals.

• Grief takes time. It can't be hurried to an end. Just as healing of the body proceeds at its own pace, so does healing of the mind.

• You will survive grief, even if at times you doubt it. Don't give up! It will pass!

Heavenly Lord, give me a calm mind and a patient trust in your healing. Amen.

FACING YOUR LOSS AND ITS PAIN

If we are to come to terms with grief successfully, there are certain tasks that we must complete.

First, we must accept the facts of our loss. This seems an unnecessary statement to make, but unfortunately this task is often the hardest work of all. For example, a grieving mother, who has experienced a caesarean and found the baby stillborn, may accuse others of lying about her dead child. Parents of a congenitally handicapped child may refuse to accept that their seemingly healthy, physically attractive child is mentally retarded.

Once the facts of the loss have been accepted, we must then allow ourselves to experience the pain of the loss. This is the period of grief most recognizable to the outside world. Displays of emotion and withdrawal are common. The degree to which society accepts outward grief will often depend on the object of that grief. For example, other people are often less ready to accept displays of grief over a change of job or a loss of potential family through infertility.

Lord, help me face my loss honestly, and uphold me through its pain. Amen.

Returning to Normal Life

Somewhere among the pain, we who are grieving will move hesitantly toward the next task. In this task we must readjust to a world where the person or object we have lost is not present. We begin to return to activities that provide some normalcy in our lives. At times we will re-experience our pain, but eventually our lives focus on new areas.

This stage heralds the final task of grieving. Our life energy will finally be directed to an attainable reality and a new goal. We begin to make a new future for ourselves.

These tasks are generally undertaken in the above order. They appear straightforward when written down, but the time taken to accomplish them can vary from weeks to months to years or even a lifetime.

It is easy to outline tasks of grieving on paper. It is not so easy to convey just how much emotion and energy are involved in working through them, and just how unclear is the distinction between the end of one and the beginning of another phase.

Heavenly Lord, in your hands are my life and future. Let your will be done. Amen.

Common Grief Experiences We Go Through

Dr. Elisabeth Kübler-Ross, in her work *On Death and Dying*, completed perhaps the most inspirational work on grieving. Although it deals with patients who were terminally ill, her work on what she termed the "stages of grieving" can be applied to other situations of loss as well.

These stages of grieving do not necessarily follow sequentially. People may drift from one stage to another, or return to a prior stage. They may even experience two stages simultaneously. We are looking at varied situations and varying intensities of grief, and so we shall concentrate less on the stages of a definite grieving process, and rather view them as common experiences in grief.

Kübler-Ross's stages of grief are:

1. Shock and denial
2. Anger
3. Bargaining
4. Depression
5. Acceptance

We shall consider these stages in the above order, recognizing that individual patterns may differ. Your experiences are as valid as anyone else's.

Lord, stay with me as I travel through this journey of grief. Amen.

The Reaction of Shock

Most commonly, the first reaction to news of a loss is shock. The mind and body seem to shut down almost completely. They are numb. Perhaps the body fails to move, thoughts become jumbled, and reactions may appear unusual. It is believed that this may be initially the mind's way of coping with a situation that would otherwise destroy the person. The mind seems to throw up a barrier against the news to try to maintain some equilibrium.

Time may pass in a disorganized sense of unreality. We may appear to function normally, but our behavior is simply a mechanical process devoid of real understanding. It is not a time when we can assimilate too much reality, too much information. It is a bit like a "living death." We feel that we can begin to understand somewhat those patients in our mental health institutions in a catatonic depressive stage, divorced from reality.

At this stage we may appear devoid of the "symptoms" of grieving. We may shed no tears. We can't yet accept the reality of the situation.

Lord Jesus, help me remember that whatever I may experience, you are still there to love me. Amen.

The Reaction of Denial

It sometimes happens that a couple who lose a child in childbirth at first refuse to see their child or sign essential papers.

Denying existence of a situation as a means of defending the psyche from anxiety is known as a defense mechanism. It is perhaps one of the more extreme of these mechanisms, but can still provide an effective buffer against strong emotional pain. It is important for those close to the grieving person to realize that denial is not necessarily a destructive thing. It is not helpful to try to force the griever to acknowledge the facts before he or she is ready. When the mind is ready to cope, denial will generally fade.

It is not uncommon for someone faced with test results indicating a serious disease to seek out desperately the possibility of errors in the test or other opinions that will invalidate the diagnosis. Similarly, mothers of a stillborn infant have been known to accuse hospital staff of lying to them and of spiriting their child away.

Generally, over a period of hours or days, people move on to other different grief experiences.

Lord, give me the strength to bear my burden, knowing that I am in your loving care. Amen.

The Reaction of Anger

Anger is a very common reaction to loss, and one of the more intense. It is also an emotion complicated by our conditioning. Discouragement of outward displays of this emotion can lead to feelings of guilt in those who feel the anger.

We must realize that anger as a feeling is not wrong. It is simply a normal human emotion, as are love and sadness. If the feeling leads to violent, destructive, or damaging behavior, then it is the behavior that is wrong, not the feeling. From childhood, many of us are not taught how to deal successfully with anger. Hence, it is often unexpressed, suppressed anger, which can linger for years after the situation causing our grief has passed.

Anger can be directed against God, medical personnel, family, our husband or wife, society, our loved one who has died, and—perhaps most commonly—against ourself.

"If only I had . . ." The "if only" game leads to feelings of guilt and anger at oneself. If unresolved, these feelings become a recipe for disaster. In fact, it is believed that prolonged depression often has its roots in such unresolved anger.

Loving Lord, I cannot hide my feelings from you. Help me not to hide them from myself. Amen.

The Reaction of Bargaining

We often attempt to find someone or something to blame for a problem. We feel that this would provide an explanation for the events, and then we would have a chance of controlling the situation. Control gives us power over a disaster and a means of allowing us to believe that it is not just a chance event. If it were merely chance, we would have to face our human powerlessness and frailty—an unpleasant thought.

We generally grow up with the attitude that if we work hard enough in a situation it will be resolved in our favor. This usually appears the case in education, employment, and sport. But when we face a loss we encounter an unpleasant situation that is not within our power to change.

One means of trying to reinstate our control is to bargain. Often the bargaining is with God. We may think something like: *God, if you cure my child, I'll go to church every Sunday.*

In 1 Samuel, Hannah made a bargain with God. She promised that if God gave her a son after years of infertility, she would dedicate this son to God.

Almighty God, help me accept that there are many things not in my control, but that everything is in your loving care. Amen.

THE REACTION OF DEPRESSION

Just as the setting of a broken leg is followed by a long period of inactivity as the bone knits, so grief includes a period of mental convalescence. This is depression. The mind has finally accepted the news it wanted to avoid and now must slowly regain its equilibrium.

When we look at grieving practices of the past, we see that in many cultures mourners were forbidden to take part in joviality for a given period of time. This showed an acceptance of the fact that grieving is a long process. Of course, some situations, such as premature delivery of a child who lives or the successful treatment of a serious medical problem will be partially resolved by the favorable outcome. Yet there is often some degree of depression involved in these cases.

Other situations, such as a chronic untreatable medical condition or the birth of a severely handicapped child, may never be resolved finally, and continuous bouts of depression may result.

Lord, make me patient in my grief, and support me when I am feeling low. Amen.

Depression Is Part of the Healing Process

Depression is a turning in on oneself. Our minds need to adjust to our loss, and to do this requires most of our energy.

When we are depressed we may be preoccupied with our thoughts, fears, and even fantasies. We may not be able to find the motivation to carry out normal household or occupational duties. This lethargy of grief is very common. For example, a person may arrive home at the end of the day to find his or her spouse still in pajamas weeping. Attempts to force someone to "buck up" usually meet with failure, at least initially. Preoccupation with one's self and the loss for a time is normal.

The griever may express a strong feeling of futility and worthlessness, and display a loss of the will to go on, even to live. This is generally not a feeling to be afraid of. It is part of nature's way of making you slow down so that the healing process can be completed.

Heavenly Lord, help me put my trust in you, knowing that you love and care for me. Amen.

Varying Symptoms of Depression

The symptoms of depression differ, as do people and situations. Some people develop intense fears; they may fear symptoms of a particular disease or the death of another loved one. Others are discontent to stay at home, and become hyperactive. Still others cannot face the outside world.

Physical symptoms can include effects on nearly every system of the body. A loss of muscular power, muscle aches or spasms, nervous diarrhea, stomach cramps, headaches, and nasal congestion are just some of the possible effects on the body. Perhaps one of the most common symptoms of depression is an irregular pattern of sleep, involving continual tiredness or insomnia. Bad dreams may further hinder the ability to sleep, as the sufferer fears the dreams will recur. Lack of sleep and the use of medication can create a vicious cycle, leading to a dependence on prescribed drugs.

The depression is generally not constant, but varies in intensity. One day you may feel ready to face the world again, only to experience a return of deep depression a day, an hour, or a minute later. But eventually, in time and with support, you will move forward at a faster rate than the rate at which you drop back.

Lord, my Rock, let me cling to you. Amen.

The Reaction of Acceptance

Little by little, those who are grieving will begin to accept that they have lost something, what that loss meant to them, and that life must go on in spite of that loss.

But acceptance is not happiness! Acceptance simply occurs when we reach a stage when it doesn't hurt so much anymore, and we are able to begin to think about other things and view our loss from a different perspective.

Normally, a broken bone will eventually knit. Similarly, our grief is eventually healed. We are becoming stronger, but there will be times when we will still feel the pain again. We may feel renewed pangs on an anniversary, or at a sudden reminder of our loved one. Acceptance does not mean happiness, but it is the foundation on which new happiness can be built.

All those who suffer grief must face their own situation, their own sorrow. For some it will be short-lived, for others long-term. God has made us all different.

Thank you, Lord, for the times when life seems almost normal again. Support me when the pain returns. Amen.

THE FINAL SOLUTION IS UP TO YOU

People in their daily lives face all kinds of problems. Crises such as the loss of a spouse, unemployment, family illness, difficulties in child-bearing, marital problems, and work pressures can all produce strain on our individual coping skills.

Although others may be able to help through caring and understanding, each crisis is personal. Your feelings about, and reactions to, the crisis situation are uniquely yours. In the final analysis, the problem is yours alone, and with you lies its solution. This is a hard fact to accept.

As children, we took our pains to our parents to soothe. As adults, our pains are our own. In many cases, time and the support of others will cushion our time of crisis, and eventually it will pass. Grief is like this. Sometimes, though, we are able to assist our own crisis resolution by positive action.

Heavenly Lord, help me face my problem and grief, knowing that I am in your hands. Amen.

Your Ability to Cope with Depression

The most common and the longest-lasting reaction to a loss is some period of depression.

Your ability to cope with depression depends on many factors, such as the success you have had in coping with and resolving past crises, the amount of support available, and your personality traits. If you have resolved past crises successfully, you may suffer from a period of depression after your loss but find that it is overcome with time. But if your loss rekindles old unresolved insecurities, your present grief may be complicated and deepened.

If your loss is prolonged or never fully resolved, depression may be longer lasting, such as in situations of infertility, repeated losses, or rearing a child with a disability. In cases where some hope still remains, you may not feel the final impact of the loss fully, and hence your grieving may be delayed.

Lord, give me the strength to cope with times of depression. Amen.

Helping Yourself

When we are depressed we may not be able to change the situation that brought on the depression. Similarly, we cannot banish our depression simply by making a conscious decision to do so.

Yet, there are things that we can do to assist the healing process. At times, a depressed person is his or her own worst enemy, actually deepening the depression by engaging in negative behaviors and thoughts that could be controlled.

The most outstanding feature of depression is often a feeling of lethargy and hopelessness. It is hard for us to find the motivation to do even the simplest task. Our feelings of failure can then be deepened, as we feel that we are losing control of life in general.

Being able to feel that we are doing something to help ourselves can help raise our spirits to some extent.

Lord, I know that my health and healing are in your hands. But help me do what I can to help myself. Amen.

Adopt Good Eating Habits

People who are depressed often become haphazard about their diet. Inappropriate eating habits and the resulting physical changes can actually accentuate depression. Overeating can lead to weight problems that further erode self-esteem. Eating irregularly or consuming the wrong foods can lead to fluctuating levels of blood sugar. The loss of some essential vitamins and amino acids can affect emotional well-being.

If you are depressed you can help, rather than hinder, your recovery, by following a sensible, healthy diet and a few simple hints:

- Make sure you eat regular meals.

- Eat a good breakfast.

- Eat to satisfy hunger, not for solace.

- Avoid alcohol and tranquilizing drugs.

- Plan your diet weekly.

- Eat foods rich in complex carbohydrates and B vitamins.

- Avoid highly sugared, salted, processed, or greasy food.

- Make sure you have enough fiber.

- Avoid caffeine.

Heavenly Lord, help me appreciate my health and the good food you provide. Amen.

Maintain Regular Exercise

Exercise can help improve the functioning of a depressed person. It is not fully understood how, but it is believed that exercise may cause hormonal changes in the body. It may increase the beta-endorphins, the mood-affecting chemicals of the brain; and it may improve the functioning of the autonomic nervous system. Benefit may also result from the feeling of taking some control of your life and the diversion from depressing thoughts that exercise offers. Exercise also enhances the circulatory system, the skin, the hair, and the physique, thereby helping to bolster self-esteem.

It is important to have a full medical checkup and to get advice from a recognized instructor before undertaking a program of exercise. Exercise performed in a social setting, including various sports, may also help you by making you feel involved with others.

General exercise that concentrates on the areas of the body most prone to stress can relieve tension.

Lord, help me help myself by caring for my body through regular exercise. Amen.

Procedures to Enhance Sleep

When we are depressed, sleep is often disrupted and daylight hours are often accompanied by feelings of tension in the mind and the muscles of the body. To overcome such problems, many depressed persons and even doctors have come to rely on prescribed drugs. Unfortunately, rather than relieve depression, these simply treat a symptom, and should never be considered as a long-term solution for depression.

Here are a few suggestions that may encourage sleep and make it possible to avoid sleeping pills.

- Do not eat a heavy meal just before bed.

- Stop worrying about falling asleep; adopt the attitude that if you don't sleep tonight there is always tomorrow.

- Take a relaxing lukewarm bath.

- Drink a glass of warm milk, rather than tea, coffee, or alcohol.

- Make sure your bedroom is quiet, dark, and well ventilated.

- Do something dull and soothing, rather than stimulating, before bed.

- Practice a relaxation technique before sleep.

Heavenly Lord, help me cast my cares on you and sleep in peace. Amen.

Asking Questions and Rethinking Attitudes

At times, when we are depressed, our thoughts can be our own worst enemies, sinking us further and further into feelings of hopelessness. We may need to ask ourselves some important questions and rethink some of our attitudes.

• How much is your attitude affected by what other people think? Do you have an image, determined by society, of what your family or marriage or situation in life ought to be? You are no less a person for being in a different situation from what some others may expect.

• Are you living in the past or in the future, rather than in the present? Your actual future may not be any better or worse than the future you imagine, only different. But it cannot be better by clinging stubbornly to unrealistic dreams.

• Are you trying to force answers to unanswerable questions? Looking for reassurances and causes is a part of grieving, but if they begin to preoccupy us, we are only hurting ourselves. Eventually we have to accept that the question *Why me?* doesn't have an answer.

• Are you making the lives of others you love more difficult by your prolonged depression? Can you also begin to consider their needs?

Lord, help me face my situation realistically. Amen.

Medication and Retaking Control of Your Life

It is common for doctors to prescribe antidepressant medication for persons experiencing depression. Research shows that such drugs are often useful for relieving depression in the short term at least. But what must be avoided is the tendency to prescribe such drugs indiscriminately without knowing and taking account of the needs and circumstances of the patient and discussing possible long-term effects.

Taking some action of your own can help overcome depression, although it is difficult when depressed to have the confidence to make changes that you feel are desirable. But it is important that you come to take control of your own life.

You can begin to be assertive by realizing that you have a right to express yourself. Ask for what you need. Be honest. Make your own decisions. If you state your requests honestly and without demanding, most people will be happy to listen. If they react negatively, that is their problem, not yours.

Heavenly Lord, I know that you love me. Help me have the confidence to be honest in expressing my needs to others. Amen.

FRIENDSHIPS AND ACTIVITIES

Other people may be able to help you in your struggle to overcome depression.

Those who have experienced a similar loss are often best able to understand the feelings of depression. Such people generally have a great deal of patience with others who are struggling with a difficult situation similar to one they have endured. It can be very reassuring to a depressed person not to have to explain his or her feelings to another, but rather to be understood implicitly.

A person facing a crisis is often changed by this situation. Relationships can change. Some are enhanced; others become strained. You may need to find new friends who are able to fulfill your needs. However, relationships need not break down when friends are sensitive and honest with each other.

Depressed persons may also need to discover other areas of life in which they are able to feel worthwhile. Success in some activity, feeling useful, and enjoying yourself can help raise your self-image.

Thank you, Lord, for the help you give me through other people. Amen.

Be Gentle with Yourself

Depression is a normal occurrence following a loss. It is nothing to be ashamed of. You are not weak because you are depressed about your situation. You have a right to feel this way.

You should feel proud that you are making moves to relieve your depression, but don't try to *force* yourself to get over it too quickly. Grief is a slow process. Even if you have a positive outlook, don't expect too much too soon. For a while you will have to accept a lower level of functioning.

It is important to live only one day, perhaps even one hour, at a time. Set yourself small goals. You may decide that today you will phone around to find out about some outside activity, or will buy a book on exercise and diet, or will go on a small outing. In the first days of depression be content to set yourself only half an hour in which to do something to relieve your depression, and be proud of achieving small goals. Larger ones will follow.

Be gentle with yourself, for you are convalescing.

Heavenly Lord, make me patient, and thankful for any small progress. Amen.

Signs of Needing Outside Help

At times some people find their grief overwhelming and are unable to cope. In some cases, present grief may be complicated by past losses or problems that have never been resolved.

In others, grief may become "stuck." A lack of support or other difficulties may see the grieving person fixed in a particular stage of grief, such as denial, anger, or depression. He or she seems unable to move through to a resolution of the grief.

Recognizing in another person grief that is abnormal (or pathological) is often difficult, but recognizing it within oneself is even more difficult. However, there are some signs, which we shall look at on the next few pages.

A lack of display of any of the characteristics of grief may indicate a problem. The person may carry on as if nothing has happened. In fact, some people become overactive while others react blandly, showing no ups or downs.

Another behavior that may point to difficulties is extreme or prolonged anger accompanied by little sadness. The griever cannot be comforted and is unable to accept rational argument.

Lord, help me live through my grief. Amen.

Further Signs of Needing Help

At times a griever's anger may be directed toward himself or herself in the form of guilt. This is particularly likely where the griever has decided, rightly or wrongly, that some action of his or hers caused the loss. Such people may hate themselves, and their self-esteem is very low. In extreme cases such guilt may lead to self-destructive behavior, based on the belief: *I have caused this. I don't deserve to live.*

In rare cases, the griever may take on symptoms of the deceased, such as breathing difficulties or chest pains. An intense fear of one's own death or that of another loved one may also be present.

Sometimes depression shows no sign of being resolved even after many months. It then interferes with the ability of the depressed person to lead a normal life.

In some cases grief does not seem to be coming to an end because unconsciously the person has denied the permanency of the loss. He or she may think, *If I keep my grief alive, my lost one may come back.*

Heavenly Lord, watch over me and protect me. Amen.

Further Signs of Needing Help

Crises can bring about changes in certain relationships, according to the level of support given during the crises. This is normal. At times, though, the griever may withdraw from all relationships and become reclusive.

Withdrawal is generally a gradual process. The person's reasons may be understandable, including the wish not to make things difficult for himself or herself, or uncomfortable for others. However, reclusive behavior will interfere with the griever's ability to function normally and will deeply affect family members from whom withdrawal is impossible without final separation.

In other cases, feelings are repressed and the person appears to be coping well with the situation. The strain remains hidden until a later time, when it is displayed in some physical disorder. Many disorders such as ulcers, some skin disorders, spastic colon, and severe headaches can be linked to underlying strain. Such symptoms may also have a physiological cause and should be referred to a doctor; one should not assume that they are due to grief alone.

Help me, Lord, in my grieving not to endanger my health or my relationships with others. Amen.

ACCEPTING THE NEED FOR HELP

The general warning signs of abnormal grieving are extreme behaviors that are prolonged, a prolonged interference with normal life, behavior that does not appear to alter with time, or behavior that changes suddenly.

Accepting another's concern or one's own concern over grieving problems can be extremely difficult. Our society has a frightening attitude toward mental health. If we are physically ill, we quickly seek help. When illness involves our mental or emotional functioning, we often deny ourselves help for fear of being labeled "crazy."

Anyone can suffer from emotional problems, particularly those who have suffered a severe loss. Yet we like to feel that we have everything under control, that we are tough. We try hard to keep up a front to fool one another, and we don't do a very good job. Addictions to drugs, food, and gambling are rampant in our society. The coronary death rate is high.

If others try to appear superior to those in emotional difficulties because they seek professional help, it is the others who have the problem, not those who are distressed.

Lord, lead me to see if and when I need help. Amen.

Where to Get Help

Many people are unsure of where to get help. Below are a few suggestions. If you are afraid to go alone or contact professional help, ask someone close to you to accompany you until you feel more at ease.

Help may be obtained from:

- One's own family.
- Local clergy, churches, and the associated caring groups.
- Local general practitioners with whom you feel comfortable. They may be able to provide support or refer you to another who may help.
- Lifeline or crisis phone line services.
- Social workers or chaplains attached to a local hospital.
- Family welfare bureaus, the Salvation Army, and other welfare organizations.
- Marriage guidance facilities.
- Government agencies, including community health centers, psychiatric clinics, and child guidance clinics.
- Private psychiatrists, psychologists, and social workers.
- Specialist support groups.

Heavenly Lord, guide me in finding the right help for my need. Amen.

Our Grief and Our Faith

During times of crisis, not only are emotional and physical capabilities strained, but so are the spiritual. When human intervention is limited or can no longer provide a solution, we look beyond the mortal to the immortal, the omnipotent, to God. People have different cultures and religions, but belief in the existence of an omnipotent one helps people make sense of their lives and the incidents that befall them, thereby giving them direction and hope.

Crises in our lives can either draw us closer to God or drive us away from God. People who have faced a crisis in which they feel powerless, such as bereavement, terminal illness, and false imprisonment, will testify to a struggle with their faith in a God who seems to allow such things to happen.

No matter how strong our faith is, none of us is immune to grief. Faith may assist us in the final resolution of grief, but it cannot prevent it.

Heavenly Lord, when I am in darkness draw me closer to you. Amen.

CRISES IN OUR FAITH

A crisis in our life can lead to a crisis in our faith. This is a common human experience. When we seem unable to control painful events in our life, doubts may arise. The pain and confusion of grief are often expressed in a crisis of faith.

It is often difficult to describe particular faith crises, for most feelings are complex, defying separation of the various elements tied together. On the following pages we shall make arbitrary separations by looking at some of the strong feelings and haunting questions that people in grief often experience.

We can't give simple answers to many of the questions or rebuild faith, for the very concept "faith" defies such a task. Faith is a confidence and a secure belief and trust in someone or something, and it is not necessarily supported by rational argument or explanation. Faith is personal, and ultimately only God himself can give us faith in him.

Lord, I know you understand me and love me even when I don't understand myself or you. Amen.

Finding an Explanation

From earliest childhood, we are taught that there is a reason for things that happen to us. A child suffers because he or she fails to do as told. *(You fell off the swing because you didn't hold on tightly enough. You failed the exam because you didn't study.)*

When things happen to us, we go looking for the reason. We may look for someone or something to blame. Even if we end up blaming the wrong thing, achieving an explanation is often more important to us than what that explanation is. When I fail an exam I can blame a teacher rather than my lack of study. This may make me feel better, even if I am only fooling myself.

Often we *can* find the cause of a problem. We can blame unemployment on the economy, or the breakdown of a relationship on our possessiveness or a partner's unfaithfulness. The solution to many such crises may lie in learning from our mistakes and taking new positive actions.

But a problem arises when we face a crisis that is beyond our control.

Heavenly Lord, help me trust in you even when I cannot understand why things happen. Amen.

Why Me, God?

Sometimes a crisis occurs in our life when the question *Why?* is not followed by a ready answer. Bereavement may be one such crisis. Suddenly our world is shattered, and we are unable to find an adequate reason. In our anger and depression of grief, we turn and ask: *Why us, God? What did we do to deserve this suffering?*

If we had been "bad," we could see this as a punishment; but when we have tried to be "good," it doesn't seem fair, particularly when so many "bad" people seem to have so few problems in their lives. Why deprive us of someone we love when others abuse their children or resent their parents or don't appreciate their husband or wife?

We are not the first to ask *Why?* of God. After Jesus' friend Lazarus had died, some people asked: "He gave sight to the blind man, didn't he? Could he not have kept Lazarus from dying?" (John 11:37).

On the cross, Jesus himself asked "Why?" of his Father: "My God, my God, why did you abandon me?" (Matthew 27:46).

Lord Jesus, you know what it is like to be grief-stricken and lonely. Be with me. Amen.

BELIEVERS ALSO SUFFER

*O*ften the answer to our *Why?* does not come immediately, or it may remain obscure. There are many questions we just do not know the answer to, although people have speculated.

Perhaps God, after giving human beings a free will and providing the processes of nature, then normally limits his intervention in these processes. Perhaps God causes or allows certain things to happen to lead us in a new direction according to his plan. Sometimes crises may be sent to test or strengthen our faith. Some people believe that we have no right to question God's ways, because his ways are perfect.

We do know that we are not alone in facing crises. Christians are just as likely to face a crisis as other people. Faith is not a magic protection. If faith promised that there would be no suffering, only joy, would there be anyone who would not cash in on such a ticket to Paradise? Suffering, like death, is no respecter of wealth, social class, previous suffering, sex, age—or religious faith.

Lord, help me cling to you, even though I don't know why you permit some things to happen. Amen.

LIFE IS NOT FAIR!

We were never promised that life would be fair!

The belief that life should be fair comes from us human beings; it makes us feel safe and secure in a world that we can then understand and control. Perhaps the question *Why me, God?* should rather be *Well, why not me?* We must accept the fact that in some situations we do not have control of events.

Such acceptance does not mean that we must be pessimistic. We may not be in control, but in God we have a powerful friend who makes many promises. One of his promises is that, though at times events seem out of control, they are actually in wiser and more powerful hands than ours: "Look at the birds flying around: they do not sow seeds, gather a harvest and put it in barns; yet your Father in heaven takes care of them! Aren't you worth much more than birds?" (Matthew 6:26).

We may lose the security of controlling our lives, yet we can have a new security in realizing that God has not abandoned us and never will, even in the darkest times.

Heavenly Lord, keep reminding me that you always care for me. Amen.

What Has Happened to My Faith?

Faith is not just a feeling; it also involves the intellect and a commitment.

Sometimes after a disappointment, when depression is our constant companion, our feelings become blunted. That spiritual "high" can be replaced by a blandness of feeling, and we may begin to doubt our faith. We feel anything but content, secure, and uplifted; instead, there is anger and sadness. Faith seems to have disappeared, and prayers become hollow and almost impossible to formulate.

For the devout, this can then lead to guilt for having such feelings: "I tell others in trouble to have faith and pray. But now it's my turn, and look what's happened to me. What kind of Christian am I?"

No matter how hard we try to recapture those feelings of serenity, the feelings of being rejected and deserted remain. This is grief, and this is normal for human beings.

Lord, strengthen my faith; hold me in your loving arms even when I can't feel your presence. Amen.

COMMITMENT RATHER THAN FEELINGS

Our relationship with God is in some ways like a marriage relationship.

In marriage, the honeymoon feeling wears off in time. The couple no longer feel the same exhilaration of being "in love." This is frightening to some people. Yet once the honeymoon is over, the real binding of marriage takes over.

This commitment is often more a matter of the intellect and will than of the emotions. The husband and wife each look carefully at their partner and clarify in their minds the reasons they love her or him and have married. They see the good and bad points more realistically. They must then work at developing the skills of communication, caring, and friendship that keep a marriage alive for a lifetime. Considered actions must be combined with the emotional high of love. At times it is determined commitment alone that keeps a marriage together over the rough patches.

Faith is similar to marriage. When the feelings are missing, faith has not disappeared. It just needs to be consciously maintained and affirmed until the feelings return. God's care for us doesn't depend on our feelings.

Lord, help me keep trusting in you, even through difficult times. Amen.

You Don't Have to "Feel Right" to Pray

Prayer is not only the formal words said while in a reverent position with closed eyes and folded hands. Our conversation with God can go on continuously, anywhere and at any time. The apostle Paul said: "Pray at all times" (1 Thessalonians 5:17).

Prayer is not always a pious, respectful activity. Prayer also includes the screaming in depression and desperation. Even the words "I can't pray Lord! I've got no faith left!" are prayer.

Prayer is discussing your feelings with God, even when you feel anger and resentment toward God. God is not frightened and upset by your anguish. The psalmist wrote: "Even if I go through the deepest darkness, I will not be afraid, Lord, for you are with me" (Psalm 23:4).

Even if the feelings are gone, faith hasn't gone. God understands. When we pour out our hearts to him in prayer, "he will be gentle to those who are weak, and kind to those who are helpless" (Matthew 12:20).

"We know that in all things God works for good with those who love him, those whom he has called according to his purpose" (Romans 8:28).

Heavenly Lord, "I do have faith but not enough. Help me to have more!" (Mark 9:24). Amen.

Feeling Anger Against God

Grief often includes anger, and who better to feel angry at than a God who has let this thing happen? As a child throws a tantrum for a parent who refuses a request, we can feel angry at this God who professes to love us but then deprives us of someone or something so important to us.

Job, in Old Testament times, knew those feelings of desertion by a God who was supposed to be loving. He lost his family and his health, and even his friends turned against him and accused him of doing wrong. In desperation and anger he cried out:

"If my troubles and griefs were weighed on scales, they would weigh more than the sands of the sea, so my wild words should not surprise you. Almighty God has pierced me with arrows, and their poison spreads through my body. God has lined up his terrors against me" (Job 6:1-4).

Those who have lost a loved one or experienced some other apparently meaningless disaster in their lives can understand Job's feelings, and similarly feel anger at a God who has done this to them.

Lord, keep loving me, and don't abandon me when I feel hurt and angry and confused. Amen.

Working Through Our Anger

It is natural for us to feel anger in a crisis, including anger against God. But if we do not resolve this anger successfully, our faith can be destroyed, and anger toward God may remain with us all our lives.

This may happen when this anger toward God is stifled by our own reactions or those of others. Some people fear that their being angry with God may provoke God to do something worse to them than has already occurred, so they suppress their outward anger. Others may discourage anger by saying "You mustn't say that!" or "You don't really mean that!" Yet suppression of anger does not make the feeling go away. Even if we suppress it outwardly, we cannot hide it from God.

Anger is a normal emotion, which is only a problem when we deal with it in such a way as to hurt others. God understands and accepts our anger. God will listen quietly while we scream and protest, and be ready to comfort us when our anger is spent. Often our anger is not really at God, but at the situation; God just "catches it."

Lord, help me not hide from myself or from you. Amen.

Is This Really Part of God's Plan?

Many Christians try to comfort a grieving person with words such as "It's God's will" or "He knows what he's doing. It's part of his plan."

Accepting that your life is mapped out in front of you is comforting when all your dreams are coming true. But when suddenly your dream, and seemingly your whole life, are shattered, the thought of a preordained plan can be frightening. It can be a depressing thought to which one can simply become resigned without hope. One then develops a fatalistic outlook and becomes depressed. Life can become viewed as something to be endured rather than enjoyed.

God seems to hold out hope by promising to hear our prayers: "And so I say to you: Ask, and you will receive; seek, and you will find; knock, and the door will be opened to you" (Luke 11:9).

God promises to answer prayer. But we can still be disappointed if we forget that Yes is not the only possible answer; No and Wait are also answers.

Heavenly Lord, teach me patience, hope, and trust. Amen.

God Promises to Hear Us

When we pray, God sometimes answers "No" or "Wait awhile." In fact, Jesus received a firm "No" in Gethsemane as he asked God if he could be relieved of his impending suffering and death.

At the present time in our life, without the advantage of hindsight, the way ahead may look dark. Yet we have been given some important promises:

• Trust in the Lord with all your heart. Never rely on what you think you know. Remember the Lord in everything you do, and he will show you the right way (Proverbs 3:5, 6).

• I alone know the plans I have for you, plans to bring you prosperity and not disaster, plans to bring about the future you hope for. Then you will call to me. You will come and pray to me, and I will answer you (Jeremiah 29:11, 12).

• God keeps his promise, and he will not allow you to be tested beyond your power to remain firm (1 Corinthians 10:13).

• Take my yoke and put it on you, and learn from me, because I am gentle and humble in spirit; and you will find rest. For the yoke I will give you is easy, and the load I will put on you is light (Matthew 11:29, 30).

Help me, Lord, to trust in you when the way is dark. Amen.

Is God Really All-Powerful?

I asked God to save my loved one, and he didn't. If he isn't cruel, maybe he just isn't as powerful as I always believed. These and similar doubts can creep into our mind when we are grieving. If God can help others, why can't he change this situation? If he made the world, surely he can look after me? Did he use up all his power on others?

In wrestling with these questions, we may react in a number of different ways. If God is all-powerful, perhaps we can make a deal with him. Part of grief can be this bargaining: "God, if you make things come out all right for me, I'll go to church regularly and give regular offerings to the church for the rest of my life."

A second reaction involves asking for our needs in prayer: "If God isn't all-powerful, then even if I ask, he may not be able to help me next time either." We may become afraid of being victims of chance.

Lord, help me believe that you know best and that you can help me. Amen.

We Don't Always Understand God's Ways

The psalmist had doubts about God's power to help: "Will the Lord always reject us? Will he never again be pleased with us? Has he stopped loving us? Does his promise no longer stand? Has God forgotten to be merciful? Has anger taken the place of his compassion?" Then I said, "What hurts me most is this—that God is no longer powerful" (Psalm 77:8-10).

Yet God *is* all-powerful. Jesus reassures us: "For God everything is possible" (Matthew 19:26).

We doubt his power when it does not seem directed toward granting our wishes. Yet at night, when the sun disappears from view, we don't doubt its power. Similarly, God's power still exists in our lives, even when things appear out of control. It may simply be present in a different form. Rather than fulfilling our wishes, his power may be present through his giving us the ability to cope with our pain and to grow as people, and perhaps to help others.

God's power is not limited. Only our vision of it is limited.

Heavenly Lord, lead and guide me according to your will. Amen.

How Do You See God?

Our view of God is often as individual as we are. Yet, our particular view can affect our coping with crises in our faith. If we see God as an angry or cruel God, then a disaster in our lives will be seen as punishment for some evil of the past or simply as an act of cruelty. Faith is then based on fear. Such a view leaves us with a faith of little joy. It seems strange that such a cruel God would allow his Son to be given as a sacrifice for mortals for whom he cares so little.

Others see a just God totaling up our good and bad points and awarding blessings according to our balance sheet. With such a God we may be able to bargain! *The better or more moral the life I lead, the less chance there is of such a terrible event happening in my life again.*

Yet others see a loving God who is a friend providing comfort in sorrow, yet who is limited in power. They feel that they must still look for control in their life. They ask for help, but worry and act impulsively, indicating their doubt in God's ability to help.

Lord, remind me that you are truly God. Amen.

Is Your God Big Enough?

Do we want a God who fits into our pocket, to be called on only when we need him to perform some magic trick? Do we demand a God over whom we have some control and who will conform to *our* plan for our lives? Most of us, if we are honest, do want such a God!

This picture of a God who is dependent on our whims is actually a gross distortion of reality. The real picture is probably more of us: a tiny, screaming, sulking, tantrum-throwing creature, standing and beating away at the ankle of a huge, omnipotent presence, who with infinite patience and love waits until we exhaust ourselves. When we are at the point of collapse, he stoops down and picks up up, giving us new strength. The view through his eyes then becomes clearer to us than it looked from the depths of our depression.

God is in control of the world and of us, and he loves us, even if we must accept that we may never fully understand his reasoning or his ways.

Heavenly Father, strengthen my faith in you as my almighty and loving God. Amen.

Suffering Is a Part of Life

Suffering is not new or unique to us. It is part of the human condition. When God took on our human nature in the man Jesus Christ, he also took on suffering.

Suffering comprises the low points in our lives, which provide a point of comparison for the high points. If our whole lives on earth were filled only with happiness we would become apathetic and selfish. What would we have to look forward to? How would we learn gratitude?

These questions may sound flippant or overly philosophical, but they are not meant to sound this way. Such insights come out of a recognition and acceptance of the changes and growth that have occurred in our own lives and those of others. Suffering has an aspect that is missing from times of happiness. Suffering forces us to accept changes and adapt to these changes.

Lord, let me not be defeated by my time of suffering, but help me benefit from it. Amen.

Growth Through Suffering

Some people are defeated by suffering, and they become bitter and afflicted for life. This is sad, but such a defeat does not make these persons less deserving of respect. Their life experiences have generally not equipped them for the fight back from defeat.

For those able to triumph over suffering, there is growth as persons. Most triumph not by reversing the condition that caused their suffering, but rather by modifying their attitude to make the changes work for them. Rather than use emotional energy in prolonged bitterness that is eventually self-destructive, they use this energy to forge new trails toward self-fulfillment.

Many become involved in helping others similarly affected. A new sensitivity to the feelings and needs of others is often noted in those who have suffered. They also experience new feelings of closeness to family, friends, and strangers who have been able to give support during their crisis.

Heavenly Lord, help me grow closer to you and be more understanding of others. Amen.

TRIUMPH OVER SUFFERING

Many who triumph over suffering develop a deeper sense of the meaning of life, and God's presence and plan, and hence a sense of contentment. By being able to accept the precarious balance of life and death, many people find greater, not less, peace with life. They find confidence in realizing that they found the necessary strength to cope with one crisis and will be able to do so in the future if need be.

The ability to triumph and gain from suffering involves hard work on the part of each individual. It is not a condition one would choose voluntarily! It is part of life for all! Whether suffering comes in the loss of a loved one, loneliness, illness, unemployment, or other circumstances, it is common to all.

Each person must bear his or her own burden of suffering. Yet, others can stand by us with their support. And God himself, who has suffered for us, is also always there to suffer with us and finally deliver us.

Thank you, Lord, for your Son Jesus Christ, who suffered for me and for all people. Amen.

After you have suffered for a little while, the God of all grace, who calls you to share his eternal glory in union with Christ, will himself perfect you and give you firmness, strength, and a sure foundation (1 Peter 5:10).